Eugene V. Debs: The Life and Legacy of America's Most Famous Socialist Political Leader

By Charles River Editors

About Charles River Editors

Charles River Editors provides superior editing and original writing services across the digital publishing industry, with the expertise to create digital content for publishers across a vast range of subject matter. In addition to providing original digital content for third party publishers, we also republish civilization's greatest literary works, bringing them to new generations of readers via ebooks.

Sign up here to receive updates about free books as we publish them, and visit Our Kindle Author Page to browse today's free promotions and our most recently published Kindle titles.

Introduction

Eugene V. Debs

"When great changes occur in history, when great principles are involved, as a rule the majority are wrong." – Eugene V. Debs

History is full of tales of men who were in the right place at the right time and thereby rose to greatness, but rarely is the story told of a man who was in the right place at the wrong time. The life of Eugene V. Debs is such a tale.

Debs was born in Middle America just before the outbreak of the Civil War, and had he been born a century later, or in a large city on one of the coasts, his story might have been much different. As he grew, he had the restlessness that often indicates greatness, but he lacked the crisis that might have allowed him to hone and use his leadership skills. He saw the needs of those less fortunate around him, and at first, like so many others, he thought that he could work within the system to correct them. However, when he ultimately concluded that he could best serve others through firebrand speeches and increasingly controversial actions, he was unable to convince enough people to follow him to make the massive changes he desired. Instead, he found himself thwarted time and again by those with more power and more established views.

Of course, this is not to discount the profound impact Debs had on the country; after all, he was one of the most famous men in America during the late 19th and early 20th century. Indeed, he was able to give to the nation a new understanding of the values and power of industrial workers, helping organize them into some of the first industrial unions in the country. He also taught the men themselves to think as a unit, and to act with a united front that allowed them to make their voices heard and to earn for themselves and their families a living wage and benefits commiserate with their work's value. As one early 20th century socialist put it, "Something was in Debs, seemingly, that did not come out unless you saw him. I'm told that even those speeches of his which seem to any reader indifferent stuff, took on vitality from his presence. A hard-bitten socialist told me once, "Gene Debs is the only one who can get away with the sentimental flummery that's been tied onto Socialism in this country. Pretty nearly always it gives me a swift pain to go around to meetings and have people call me 'comrade.' That's a lot of bunk. But the funny part of it is that when Debs says 'comrade' it is all right. He means it. That old man with the burning eyes actually believes that there can be such a thing as the brotherhood of man. And that's not the funniest part of it. As long as he's around I believe it myself."

In the course of his work, Debs also changed the political scene in America. He established the Socialist Party, and when he ran for president in 1912, he attracted a noticeable percentage of the popular vote. No Socialist politician has been as successful on the national level before or since. However, even as he garnered popularity, the times in which he lived hampered his work, for the outbreak of World War I, along with the Bolshevik Revolution in Russia, brought socialism under suspicion. Most controversially, Debs was arrested and imprisoned during World War I on charges of sedition, and while that episode has justly marred President Woodrow Wilson's legacy, prison damaged Debs' health even as his spirit strove on for one last victory. In many ways, his end seems tragic, but for those who benefited through the years from his practical work for organized labor and his theoretical work for socialism, his death marked neither a tragedy nor an end, just a new type of beginning.

Eugene V. Debs: The Life and Legacy of America's Most Famous Socialist Political Leader chronicles the life and work that made him one of America's most influential men. Along with pictures of important people, places, and events, you will learn about Debs like never before.

Debs' Early Years

"For myself, I want no advantage over my fellow man, and if he is weaker than I, all the more is it my duty to help him." - Debs

Eugene Victor Debs was born in Terre Haute, Indiana, on November 5, 1855. His parents, Jean and Marguerite Debs, had come to America from Colmar, Alsace in France during the first major immigration wave of the 19th century. The family had a comfortable, upper middle-class existence supported by Jean's success in businesses, most notably a meat market and a local textile mill. The family was educated, and Debs was named for the famous French authors Eugène Süe and Victor Hugo.

Süe

Hugo

In spite of his family's prosperity, young Debs was a happy but restless child, as biographer Wayne Morgan observed: "Public life and the glamor of the outside world were far from his youthful thoughts; his first problem was making a living. The boy was drawn to the railroaders like steel filings to a magnet, but his father frowned on such ambitions. The Debs family had followed a long, hard road to respectable middle-class prosperity, and the elder Debs wanted his sons to make their mark in a profession. He himself had worked at many jobs, and suffered all the tortures and frustrations that beset the immigrant, settling at last to ownership of a small grocery store in Terre Haute. He was a kindly, gentle man, who exercised a great influence on his eldest son. A wide reader and avid social critic, he impressed upon the young Eugene the necessity of understanding the world around him…The restlessness of adventure was in his blood; the railroad was too close, its whistle too intriguing to allow him to count cookies and measure cloth for housewives. He devoted much of his excess energy to reading, and read widely if not deeply, drinking at the same fountains as his father, filled early with the rhetoric and reasoning of social protest and the romantic view of life."

Ultimately, Debs rebelled against his parents' hope for his future, dropping out of school when he was only 14 years old so that he could take a job with the Vandalia Railroad. There he worked for 50 cents a day, cleaning the black grease off freight engines. In spite of his lack of interest in education, Debs was a hard worker and was soon promoted to work in the railroad shops, where he cleaned and painted trains being brought in for repair and servicing. Just after his 16th birthday, the train company promoted Debs to night fireman on a locomotive, where he worked stoking the engines of trains running through the dark Indiana countryside with loads of materials and passengers. Morgan noted, "It was not an easy life even for the lean, hardened young man. Bad weather, poor equipment, erratic schedules and the unforeseen combined with low wages and long hours to make the railroaders a tough group. Drinking, gambling, and the roughest horseplay were their pastimes. The young Debs entered into all of this gladly. He found in the men around him a hard core of principle, a feeling of camaraderie inspired by common hardships, and he greatly admired their courage, sense of honor, and general outlook. He made many lasting friendships, each of which strengthened his belief that men were basically good and that evil was the product of the social system, rather than human nature."

In February 1875, Debs joined the Brotherhood of Locomotive Firemen (BLF). Founded in 1873, the BLF was a combination of trade union and "fraternal benefit society," an organization that provided both social and economic support to its members. Such organizations were widespread in the late 19th century in an era before the government provided social safety nets. In its fraternal functions it was not unlike the Knights of Columbus, which was founded about the same time, but in its union activities, it was much different.

As is often the case, maturity and hard work led young Debs to see that an education might actually hold more value than he originally thought. Thus, in July 1875, he left the railroad business to work at a wholesale grocery house, and this job's regular hours allowed him to attended business school at night.

Upon completion of his studies, he decided to enter local politics. Debs was first elected as the City Clerk for Terre Haute, a position in which he served from 1879-1883. The following year, Terre Haute's Democrats helped him becogetme elected to the Indian General Assembly, but Debs served only one term. Morgan explained, "Debs allowed the Democrats to run him for the state legislature in 1884. Thinking that he could help his union followers, and utterly unaware of the political process, he plunged into public life again. In 1885, he maneuvered a bill through the lower house providing that railroads compensate their employees when injured through no fault of their own. The bill died a lingering death in the upper house and the experience was such a shock to Debs that he refused to run for re-election, feeling that he had failed his followers. He turned from party politics and never afterwards had any faith in parliamentary process under the old parties."

A Labor Activist

Debs as a young man

"Ten thousand times has the labor movement stumbled and fallen and bruised itself, and risen again; been seized by the throat and choked and clubbed into insensibility; enjoined by courts, assaulted by thugs, charged by the militia, shot down by regulars, traduced by the press, frowned upon by public opinion, deceived by politicians, threatened by priests, repudiated by renegades, preyed upon by grafters, infested by spies, deserted by cowards, betrayed by traitors, bled by leeches, and sold out by leaders, but notwithstanding all this, and all these, it is today the most vital and potential power this planet has ever known, and its historic mission of emancipating the workers of the world from the thraldom of the ages is as certain of ultimate realization as is the setting of the sun." – Debs, 1904

Though no longer working for the railroad, Debs still retained his membership in the BLF and remained active in the organization. As a result, he served as a delegate from Terre Haute to the organization's national convention in 1877, and the year after that, he became the associate editor of the *Firemen's Magazine*, the monthly newsletter for the national organization. A few years later, in 1880, he became the Grand Secretary and Treasurer for the organization and was also promoted to editor of the magazine. He retained these positions until the early 1890s. Morgan remarked, "Throughout the 1880's he worked steadily to build up the union, devoting time, health, money to the cause. He worked eighteen hours a day, full of idealism as well as the practical belief that he could help his men. At that time he knew little if anything of socialism and was committed to the craft unionism which he vehemently condemned in a few years."

Even before Debs' own ideology began evolving, the BLF provided an early training ground for him, allowing him to consider and clarify his views on labor and unions within a rather conservative organization. In the 1880s, the members of the BLF were more inclined to organize a company picnic than a strike; in fact, never once in the organization's early history did its members formally vote to strike. This was important to Debs, who focused most of his attention during his early career on social programs that would help BLF members, specifically in establishing an insurance program that would provide death and disability benefits to the families of stricken members. He also wrote editorials demanding that each man look after himself and work hard to make the most of his opportunities. In his mind, this meant that they should avoid heavy drinking, being idle, and lying. He also believed that workers should offer their employers an honest day's work for an honest day's pay.

Obviously these values sat well with the railroad companies, who supported the BLF and encouraged men to organize locally. They also allowed their leaders certain special privileges, like free railroad tickets to and from their conventions. Debs in turn praised the railroads' leadership, and he even invited Henry C. Lord, president of the famed Atchison, Topeka and Santa Fe Railroad, to write for the *Firemen's Magazine* in March 1883. In an article entitled, "Gratitude and Ingratitude," Lord asserted, "Gratitude is always allied to courage, it is the twin brother or sister, as the case may be. What heart, not absolutely rotten with selfishness, does not fairly leap forth in love and gratitude…The life of every man brought much in contact with the world and all sides and crooks, heights, depths and corners of human nature is of necessity a checkered one and full of instruction." It is difficult to say what was on Lord's mind when he wrote this, but he and Debs would soon find themselves on opposite sides over who should be grateful, and for what.

On June 9, 1885, Debs made one of the most monumental and least understood decisions of his life when he married Kate Metzel. Even in the 21st century, she is often maligned, partially because their relationship, or at least the public conception of it, has been shaped by Irving Stone's biographical novel, *Adversary in the House*. In that book, Stone portrayed Debs' "tempestuous relationship with a wife who rejects the very values he holds most dear." Metzel inherited a notable amount of wealth from family members, and she openly spent it in ways that contrasted with her husband's advocacy on behalf of the lower classes, which would indirectly expose him to criticism.

On the other hand, recent scholarship by researcher Micki Morahn tells a different story. According to Morahn, "They were real partners. ... That's one of the things that brought Gene and Kate together - this intellectual interest. They were both looking for that person who you could sit down with at the end of the day and share your deepest thoughts…She helped him in many ways that aren't expressed in the biographies…It was a true marriage of equals."

Kate Metzel Debs

The Eugene V. Debs Foundation's picture of Debs' house in Terre Haute

According to journalist Mark Bennett, who interviewed Morahn in 2018, "Kate's ability to join Gene on travels across the country and abroad was indeed limited once her widowed mother, Katherine, and later young nephew, Oscar Baur Jr., moved into the Debses' Terre Haute home. Kate was tending to live-in relatives for the first two decades of the 20th century - the prime period of Gene's political activity. Yet, she managed to join Gene on stage at Evansville for a campaign speech during his 1908 run for the presidency. Kate also rode with him that year aboard the Red Special, his campaign train, as it stopped for rallies in numerous cities on a route from New York to Terre Haute...During Gene's years as a union activist on behalf of railroad workers in the late-1800s, Kate traveled with him to conventions and meetings at Philadelphia, New Orleans, Atlanta, Nashville and California."

Certainly, the early years of their marriage were difficult ones, for Debs' ideas were evolving in a much more radical direction than he had considered in the past. This move away from the idea that management and labor could be friendly developed slowly, but it began to become obvious around the time of the Burlington Railroad Strike in 1888. Writing in 1930, historian McAlister Coleman explained, "In February, 1888, the C. B. & Q. engineers, who were receiving the lowest wages paid by any road running into Chicago, struck for a raise. They were promptly joined in their demands by the scoopers, and for the first time in his life, P. M. Arthur found himself signing what amounted to an ultimatum. In his demand for better wages and conditions he was joined by the Grand Master of the firemen. [Eu]Gene [Debs], scenting the battle from afar, packed up his bag again and went out to tell the strikers to stick to a triumphant end. He was so exhilarated with the revival of militancy that he actually praised Arthur for his 'courage and modesty.'"

Later, according to Coleman, an exchange took place along these lines:

> Arthur: "Debs, we have got to get the switchmen out."
>
> Debs: "Sure. Why don't you call them out?"
>
> Arthur: "They won't come…because when the switchmen strike not one of your aristocratic engineers will do so much as get off his engine."

While Debs was able to convince the switchmen to strike, he still did not call on his own people to do so. However, he also discouraged strikebreakers, telling one man, "You are too true a friend of the cause of labor to allow another man's errors or your own personal grievances to govern your course…No matter how leaders may err, it is your duty and mine to exert what influence we may possess to prevent organized workingmen from cutting each other's throats."

During this crisis, Debs came to realize, "The strike is the weapon of the oppressed, of men capable of appreciating justice and having the courage to resist wrong and contend for principle. The nation had for its corner stone a strike, and while arrogant injustice throws down the gauntlet and challenges the right to the conflict, strikes will come, come by virtue of irrevocable laws, destined to have a wider sweep and greater power as men advance in intelligence and independence." In an article in the *Firemen's Magazine*, he railed against "statutes made in the interests of corporations and under which they have been and are still enabled to play the role of oppressors, adding, "It matters not under what outrages employees of corporations may labor, no officer, chairman or leader of any labor organization can so much as advise resistance, without being held liable to prosecution for conspiracy, the penalty being a fine and imprisonment."

Debs also castigated the Pinkerton detectives who had been brought in to break the strike, calling them "distorted, deformed, hideous mentally and morally [men whose] trade is treason, their breath pollution and yet the officials of the C. B. & Q. formed a conspiracy with these professional liars, perjurers, forgers, cut-throats and murderers to overcome a strike, the result of a policy of flagrant injustice."

A poster made by Burlington strikers in 1888

Despite the efforts, by the time the BLF met in Atlanta, Georgia, for the annual meeting, it was obvious that the strike had failed. Coleman noted, "He decided that the time had come to risk his federation project. In it he saw a longviewed policy which, if carried through, would make any management think twice before cutting wages. The tie-up of a system from roundhouse to the farthest terminal was nothing to be sneezed at. As soon as the convention got down to business, Gene proposed that immediate steps be taken to bring into a federation the six railroad workers' organizations, the engineers, firemen, and brakemen brotherhoods, the Order of Railway Conductors, the Yardmasters' Mutual Benefit Association and the Switchmen's Mutual Aid Association. He had done his educational work well. The convention's mood was co-operative. Like Gene, the delegates had seen the disastrous effects of isolation. They set up a committee, consisting of F. P. Sargent, Grand Master of the Firemen, Vice Grand Master J. J. Hannahan and

Debs, authorized to confer with the other rail organizations."

In his next editorial, Debs crowed, "We hail with becoming satisfaction the dawn of the new era of fraternal unity which we believe the future has in store for the brotherhoods of railroad employees, and in the future, as in the past, this magazine will labor for its fullest realization." But ultimately, the strike failed, and Debs' efforts proved to be too little, too late. In the aftermath, Debs resigned as Grand Secretary for the Brotherhood in 1893 and threw himself into organizing the American Railway Union (ARU), one of the first industrial unions in America. Unlike the BLF, which was centered around one type of worker (firemen), the ARU sought to unite all workers in the same industry (railroads). It was a sharp departure from traditional unionism in America and began a decades-long tension between the craft unions and the industrial unions. Debs became the ARU's first president, and he immediately began to fight for the rights of the men whom he saw as mistreated and oppressed, taking aim right from the beginning at those in high position.

On August 31, 1893, Supreme Court Justice Henry Brown angered Debs and many others by telling the American Bar Association, "While, in this country at least, private fortunes are larger than they have ever been before, the condition of the laboring class has improved in equal ratio. There was never a time when the working classes were so well paid, or when their wages could buy for them so many of the comforts of life as now. Not only are the working man's wages higher, but his hours of labor are shorter. He is better housed, better clad, better fed, better taught, reads better and cheaper papers, sends his children to better 5 schools, and enjoys more opportunities for recreation and for seeing the world than ever before. He not only practically dictates his own hours of labor, but in large manufacturing centers he is provided with model lodging houses for his family, with libraries, parks, clubs, and lectures for his entertainment and instruction, with cheap excursion trains for his amusement on Sundays and holidays; and not only absolutely but relatively to the rich is vastly better off than he was fifty years ago."

Brown

Debs took issue with this, and he pointed out in an article in the *Firemen's Magazine* (where he remained editor through much of 1894) that Brown made these remarks "at a time when multiplied thousands of workingmen were out of employment, not knowing where they could secure a meal of victuals...But supposing no clouds overspread the skies of labor and the picture painted by the judge was literally true, then it is seen that during the past 50 years great improvements have been made in the condition of workingmen. The question arises, who brought about this improvement? ... Not rich men, but workingmen by combination, by strikes, by sacrifice, and as labor's emancipation has not yet come, and as the rich are still oppressing, and as the courts are still corrupt, labor has before it herculean tasks to perform. Hitherto the combinations of labor have been on a small scale, and imperfect. Once unified, once redeemed from the fetters of envy and jealousy, once marshaled under one banner, and they will go forth from bondage...."

A few months later, in 1894, Debs organized his first strike, this one against the Great Northern

Railway. On April 13, 1894, the railroad's general manager, C.W. Case, opened his mail and found a letter from the ARU informing him, "I am instructed by your employees to say that unless the scale of wages and rules of classes of employees that were in effect prior to the first cut made August 1, 1893, are restored and switchmen at Great Falls and Helena receive the same pay and schedules as at Butte and the management agrees to meet the representatives of the employees at Minot not later than ten days hence and formulate schedules accordingly, all classes of employees will quit work at 12 o'clock noon this 13th day of April." Obviously, it was too late by this point in time to make the changes, so the strike went forward.

The strike lasted just over two weeks, and things were heated from the beginning. According to historian David Karsner, "On April 16, members of the American Railway Union received a circular letter containing the scale of wages paid on the Great Northern lines…. The officials of the Great Northern soon learned of the circular sent to its employees, and at once sent out a cipher dispatch to its superintendents and managers to remove all agitators and those known to be in sympathy with the A. R. U. Debs and his co-officials learned of this step taken by the railroad to break down the morale of the men, and the strike was speedily called. The railroad was given no time to prepare a counter offensive. From the Butte headquarters of the A. R. U. came the appeal to the men, couched in the following vein: 'We need your financial and moral support everywhere. It is the greatest strike the world has ever seen. Give us your moral and financial support through the general office at Chicago. Act quickly. See if we cannot break the chains that are being forged to reduce us, not only to slavery, but to starvation.'"

The railroad workers responded quickly and enthusiastically, and on April 22, Debs and his ARU Vice-President, George Howard, spoke before a crowd of workers in St. Paul, Minnesota, the home of Great Northern's General Office and President James J. Hill. According to Karsner, "With imminent defeat staring him in the face, Mr. Hill called a conference of a few railroad managers and labor leaders, the main theme of his talk to them being that he would offer arbitration. When Mr. Hill had concluded, a tall, gaunt man arose in the back of the council chamber. Moving slowly to the front where Mr. Hill sat the man began to speak. It was Debs." Debs replied to Hill by telling him, "To divide the organization and make trouble between the union and the Brotherhoods. I understand such to be the policy of this company. … We presented the terms upon which we would go to work. I am authorized to say that we will settle on these terms and on no others. … Now, understand me that I am too much of a gentleman to make a threat and I do not mean this as anything but a plain statement of fact, but if there is no adjustment, those men will withdraw from your service in a body. They are convinced that their demand is a just one. If their request is not complied with they will, without regard to consequences, continue this struggle on the lines already laid down and fight it out with all the means at their command within the limits of the law. We understand your position; you understand ours. We will not withdraw from this conference. We shall be in the city several days and shall be glad to receive any further communications from you."

Karsner concluded, "The Great Northern strike was won in eighteen days and not one drop of human blood was shed. It was the first signal victory achieved by the workers in this country standing together, united, for their demands, and other trades and revived their spirits which had been all but annihilated after the Haymarket riots and hangings seven years before. Debs returned to his home in Terre Haute on May 3, 1894, and four thousand of his friends, neighbors, men, women and children, greeted him with shouts and music. He addressed his fellow citizens in a public park, near the Terre Haute House."

Hill

With this first victory securely under his belt, Debs soon became involved in the Pullman Strike of 1894. The Pullman Palace Car Company had experienced financial downturns during the Panic of 1893 and had cut its employees' wages by more than 25%. At the same time, it had continued to charge them the same amount for rent on their company houses and other services provided by the company. When the ARU met in Chicago, the members who worked for the Pullman Company and many of their allies asked the ARU to organize a boycott of the railroad. At first, Debs opposed this plan, insisting that a boycott was a risky plan, and that the ARU itself was too young and weak to take on such a large company. He was also afraid, it seems, that a serious defeat so early in its founding would be a permanent setback for the organization. However, the rank-and-file did not share his concerns and voted to refuse to work on any train carrying Pullman cars. ARU Director Martin Elliott went so far as to expand the strike to include more than 80,000 workers, forcing Debs to join in the fight or risk being branded a coward.

During this time, John Swinton, writing for the *New York Times*, covered one of Debs' rallies and compared him to Abraham Lincoln: "It seemed to me that both men were imbued with the same spirit. Both seemed to me as men of judgment, reason, earnestness and power. Both seemed to me as men of free, high, genuine and generous manhood. I took to Lincoln in my early life, as I took to Debs a third of a century later." Of course, there were significant differences between Debs' actions and those of Lincoln. The late president had sought to uphold the law of the land, at least as he and his administration saw it, while Debs was soon accused of breaking it. Also, Lincoln sought to put down a rebellion, while Debs openly favored revolution, to the point that the Pullman Strike soon became known in common circles as "Debs' Rebellion."

By July 9, even the *New York Times* had changed its tune, opining, "[Debs] is a lawbreaker at large, an enemy of the human race. There has been quite enough talk about warrants against him and about arresting him. It is time to cease mouthings and begin. Debs should be jailed, if there are jails in his neighborhood, and the disorder his bad teaching has engendered must be squelched. Gen. Miles evidently intends to squelch it. It may be a rude business, but it is well to remember that no friends of the Government of the United States are ever killed by its soldiers -- only its enemies."

At least some federal leaders agreed with the *Times*, and they obtained an injunction prohibiting the strike on the basis that it was impeding the federal mail. Grover Cleveland, then in his second term as president, infuriated Debs, who had previously supported him, by sending the U.S. Army to break the strike and serve the injunction. Violence broke out, leading to more than $80 million in property damage. 30 strikers also lost their lives, and the government worked with private companies to blacklist thousands of other men who had participated in the strike.

"GIVING THE BUTT"—THE WAY THE "REGULAR" INFANTRY TACKLES A MOB.

NATIONAL GUARDSMEN FIRING INTO THE MOB AT LOOMIS AND FORTY-NINTH STREETS, JULY 7TH.—Drawn by G. W. Peters from a Sketch by G. A. Coffin.

Contemporary depictions of violence during the strike

A picture of strikers confronting the Illinois National Guard

As for Debs, a judge found him in contempt of court for his role and sentenced him to federal prison. Debs was fortunate when it came to his defense, because young Clarence Darrow had recently left his position as counsel for a railroad company and now decided to represent someone from the other side. His case made it to the Supreme Court in 1895, and while the justices found unanimously in favor of the federal government, Debs had already served his sentence by the time the case was decided.

KING DEBS.

A cartoon criticizing Debs' role in the strike and the strike's disruption of food transportation

A Socialist Activist

"The issue is Socialism versus Capitalism. I am for Socialism because I am for humanity. We have been cursed with the reign of gold long enough. Money constitutes no proper basis of civilization. The time has come to regenerate society — we are on the eve of universal change."
– Debs, 1897

Debs emerged from jail a changed man, and he described the impact the events had on him, as well as the influences he was introduced to along the way: "The Chicago jail sentences were followed by six months at Woodstock and it was here that Socialism gradually laid hold of me in its own irresistible fashion. Books and pamphlets and letters from Socialists came by every mail and I began to read and think and dissect the anatomy of the system in which workingmen, however organized, could be shattered and battered and splintered at a single stroke. The writings of Bellamy and Blatchford early appealed to me. The ' Cooperative Commonwealth' of Gronlund also impressed me, but the writings of Kautsky were so clear and conclusive that I readily grasped, not merely his argument, but also caught the spirit of his Socialist utterance —

and I thank him and all who helped me out of darkness into light…It was at this time, when the first glimmerings of Socialism were beginning to penetrate, that Victor L. Berger — and I have loved him ever since — came to Woodstock, as if a providential instrument, and delivered the first impassioned message of Socialism I had ever heard — the very first to set 'the wires humming in my system.' As a souvenir of that visit there is in my library a volume of 'Capital,' by Karl Marx, inscribed with the compliments of Victor L. Berger, which I cherish as a token of priceless value. "The American Railway Union was defeated but not conquered — overwhelmed but not destroyed. It lives and pulsates in the Socialist movement, and its defeat but blazed the way to economic freedom and hastened the dawn of human brotherhood."

For the rest of his life, Debs would consider himself a socialist, and he would fight to expand socialism throughout the United States. He began by speaking to the leadership of the ARU in the summer of 1897 and encouraging it to join with another organization, the Brotherhood of the Cooperative Commonwealth (BCC), to found the Social Democracy of America (SDA). The BCC was even newer than the ARU, having sprung up in New England in 1895. Its constitution committed its members to the following: "1. To educate the people in the principles of Socialism; 2. To unite all socialists in one fraternal association; 3. To establish cooperative colonies and industries in one state until that state is socialized." Its third goal obviously never materialized, and in 1897, the group tried to draft Debs as a national organizer. However, Debs was too busy with strike-related issues to help the organization out at that time.

In the end, the BCC rejected Debs' offers to form join the SDA, but the SDA ultimately went on without them. In 1900, Debs ran for president under the Social Democratic Party, getting just over half a percentage point of the popular vote. Writing in the radical left-wing weekly *Appeal to Reason* just after the election, Debs warned, "The machine became more perfect day by day; is lowered the wage of the worker, and in due course of time it became so perfect that it could be operated by unskilled labor of the woman, and she became a factor in industry. The owners of these machines were in competition with each other for trade in the market; it was war; cheaper and cheaper production was demanded, and cheaper labor was demanded. In the march of time it became necessary to withdraw the children from school, and these machines came to be operated by the deft touch of the fingers of the child. In the first stage, machine was in competition with man; in the next, man in competition with both, and in the next, the child in competition with the whole combination. Today there is more than three million women engaged in industrial pursuits in the United States, and more than two million children. It is not a question of white labor or black labor, or male labor or female or child labor, in this system; it is solely a question of cheap labor, without reference to the effect upon mankind."

Debs' run for the presidency was hampered by many difficulties, and it seems impossible to think that he believed he had any chance to win. Therefore, it is perhaps more realistic to consider his actions in light of an effort to draw attention to the principles of socialism and introduce them to the American people. Unlike some, Debs was a true believer, and he thought to the core of his being that socialism offered the best future for the common American. It was to this end that he devoted the rest of his life. According to historian Philip Foner, "In 1902, and during the period between 1902 and 1904, his speeches and writings were full of references to the superiority of industrial unionism and the necessity of combining this principle with uncompromising action based upon the class struggle. His most important contribution in this period, and one of his chief theoretical works, was *Unionism and Socialism, A Plea for Both*, published in, *Appeal to Reason* in 1904 and reprinted as a pamphlet shortly thereafter...The study began with an analysis of the development of unionism. Debs then emphasized that modern industrial conditions required a modern type of unionism. 'This is the industrial plan, the modern method applied to modern conditions, and it will in time prevail.' But Debs was convinced that the [American Federation of Labor] could not be quickly converted into a modern type of union, and that a new organization was necessary."

Eventually, Debs' work began to pay off, as Foner concluded: "Debs' pamphlet did not impress the dominant elements in the Socialist Party leadership who still clung to the belief that the A.F. of L. would soon be transformed, by the education of its membership, into a revolutionary union. But it did arouse widespread discussion in radical circles. Debs' viewpoint was discussed at the Twelfth Annual Convention of the Western Federation of Miners held at Salt Lake City, during May and June 1904, and helped to crystallize the growing sentiments for a new, broad industrial union. The executive board of the W.F. of M. was instructed to take 'such action as might be necessary' to bring the representatives of organized labor together to outline plans 'for the amalgamation of the working class into one general organization'..."

Undeterred by his poor showing in 1900, Debs ran a second time for the presidency in 1904, this time on the ticket of the newly formed Socialist Party of America. He garnered 3% of the popular vote, finishing third behind the two major party candidates.

The following year, Debs organized yet another labor union, this one made up of Industrial Workers of the World (IWW). In doing so, he worked with William "Big Bill" Haywood, then the leader of the Western Federation of Miners, and Daniel De Leon, the head of the Socialist Labor Party. In their meeting, which Haywood called the "Continental Congress of the working class," Haywood proclaimed, "We are here to confederate the workers of this country into a working class movement that shall have for its purpose the emancipation of the working class from the slave bondage of capitalism. There is no organization, or there seems to be no labor organization, that has for its purpose the same object as that for which you are called together today. The aims and objects of this organization should be to put the working class in possession of the economic power, the means of life, in control of the machinery of production and distribution, without regard to capitalist masters."

Haywood

De Leon

In spite of his involvement on all levels of union organization, Debs never became completely comfortable with the role of leader. In 1906, he went so far as to say, "I am not a Labor Leader; I do not want you to follow me or anyone else; if you are looking for a Moses to lead you out of this capitalist wilderness, you will stay right where you are. I would not lead you into the promised land if I could, because if I led you in, some one else would lead you out. You must use your heads as well as your hands, and get yourself out of your present condition."

Nevertheless, Debs ran for office again in 1908, this time using his platform to lobby on behalf of fellow socialists Haywood (then standing trial for murder) and Charles Moyer, who was facing charges related to his involvement in the Colorado Labor Wars. Commenting on their situations, Debs wrote, "There have been twenty years of revolutionary education, agitation, and organization since the Haymarket tragedy, and if an attempt is made to repeat it, there will be a revolution and I will do all in my power to precipitate it. If they attempt to murder Moyer, Haywood, and their brothers, a million revolutionists at least will meet them with guns." On another occasion, he wrote in the *Appeal to Reason*, "Ferdinand Lassalle, the brilliant social revolutionist, once said that the war against capitalism was not a rose water affair. It is rather of the storm and tempest order. All kinds of attacks must be expected, and all kinds of wounds will be inflicted. You will be assailed within and without, spat upon by the very ones that you are doing your best to serve, and at certain crucial moments find yourself isolated, absolutely alone as if to compel surrender, but in those moments, if you have the nerve, you become supreme."

Moyer

Although he continued running campaigns, Debs had little respect for the political process. He derided those he called "Sewer Socialists" for pursuing and winning small public offices, insisting that the true hope for the nation lay in organized labor. In that vein, during the early 1900s, he focused most of his energy of organizing industry wide unions rather than the traditional trade unions, for he felt that there was more power to be had if an entire industry could mobilize instead of just those with a particular skill. However, he was often distracted from these goals by discontent and disagreement among the members of the IWW. According to historian Robert Hyfler, "In Debs's writing and thinking, we see a dialectical interplay between struggle, the level of consciousness, and the level of organization. As workers engage in struggle, they see the logic of a class analysis of society and the need for industrial organization. Once organized along industrial lines, workers begin to perceive and experience their common interest with other workers who do similar yet not identical work. Eventually, the interdependence of all industry (and hence the logic of socialism) becomes apparent to workers as the concept of 'class' is further crystallized in their minds. 'With each new battle,' Debs asserted, 'the trend has been steadily toward a more perfect organization and a more comprehensive grasp of its [the working class's] mighty mission.'…To the founders of the IWW, organizational factors were of such supreme importance that the success of the struggle was dependent upon them. In their analysis, struggle--however intense--carried on within a nonrevolutionary craft union could never lead to a socialist consciousness; the structure and tactics of such organizations were a direct contradiction of everything socialist. Conversely, a militant labor organization, organized along industrial lines and unwilling to sanctify through a time contract the 'rights' of the employer, embodied in its structure and tactics both the reality and the goals of the class struggle."

Sadly for Debs, Haywood led the faction of the IWW that ultimately turned its back on the political process, believing it would never serve the interests of the working class. With a heavy heart, Debs let Haywood go, refusing to cooperate with him in tactics that were often aggressive and sometimes even violent. Though he and Haywood would remain friends, they would not be comrades in the fight anymore.

The split took its toll, and in four months the Socialist Party's numbers dropped from 135,000 to 80,000, causing many Socialist incumbents to lose their seats in the 1912 election. Still, when Debs ran again for president in 1912, he garnered 6% of the popular vote. During his campaign, he wrote an article called "Why You Should Vote for Socialism," in which he told readers, "You must either vote for or against your own material interests as a wealth producer; there is no political purgatory in this nation of ours, despite the desperate efforts of so-called Progressive capitalists politicians to establish one. socialism alone represents the material heaven of plenty for those who toil and the Socialist Party alone offers the political means for attaining that heaven of economic plenty which the toil of the workers of the world provides in unceasing and measureless flow. Capitalism represents the material hell of want and pinching poverty of degradation and prostitution for those who toil and in which you now exist, and each and every political party, other than the Socialist Party, stands for the perpetuation of the economic hell of capitalism. For the first time in all history you who toil possess the power to peacefully better your own condition. The little slip of paper which you hold in your hand on election day is more potent than all the armies of all the kings of earth."

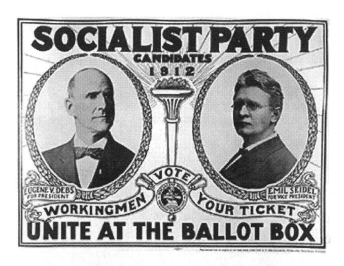

A campaign poster during the 1912 campaign

What was it that made Debs such an attractive leader? Those who heard him speak often praised his charismatic oratory, with some even comparing it to the traveling evangelists who were gaining popularity during the early years of the 20th century. This is ironic, given that Debs himself generally eschewed all forms of organized religion, considering religion to be part of the capitalist plot to keep the masses in check.

Debs also took a chance in using language associated with the rising spread of discontent in Russia, but in this instance, he got away with it. According to one of his followers, "Gene Debs is the only one who can get away with the sentimental flummery that's been tied onto Socialism in this country. Pretty nearly always it gives me a swift pain to go around to meetings and have people call me 'comrade.' That's a lot of bunk. But the funny part of it is that when Debs says "comrade" it's all right. He means it. That old man with the burning eyes actually believes that there can be such a thing as the brotherhood of man. And that's not the funniest part of it. As long as he's around I believe it myself."

World War I

"These are the gentry who are today wrapped up in the American flag, who shout their claim from the housetops that they are the only patriots, and who have their magnifying glasses in hand, scanning the country for evidence of disloyalty, eager to apply the brand of treason to the men who dare to even whisper their opposition to Junker rule in the United Sates. No wonder Sam Johnson declared that "patriotism is the last refuge of the scoundrel." He must have had this Wall Street gentry in mind, or at least their prototypes, for in every age it has been the tyrant, the oppressor and the exploiter who has wrapped himself in the cloak of patriotism, or religion, or both to deceive and overawe the people." – Debs, 1918

While it is highly unlikely that Debs would have ever won the presidency, he almost certainly would have continued to lead the fight for socialism if World War I did not break out across Europe in 1914.

From the very beginning, Debs spoke out against potential American participation in the war. On September 11, 1915, he said, "I am not opposed to all war, nor am I opposed to fighting under all circumstances, and any declaration to the contrary would disqualify me as a revolutionist. When I say I am opposed to war I mean ruling class war, for the ruling class is the only class that makes war. It matters not to me whether this war be offensive or defensive, or what other lying excuse may be invented for it, I am opposed to it, and I would be shot for treason before I would enter such a war. Capitalists wars for capitalist conquest and capitalist plunder must be fought by the capitalists themselves so far as I am concerned, and upon that question there can be no compromise and no misunderstanding as to my position. I have no country to fight for; my country is the earth; I am a citizen of the world. I would not violate my principles for God, much less for a crazy kaiser, a savage czar, a degenerate king, or a gang of pot-bellied parasites…I am opposed to every war but one; I am for the war with heart and soul, and that is the world-wide war of social revolution. In that war I am prepared to fight in any way the ruling class may make necessary, even to the barricades. There is where I stand and where I believe the Socialist Party stands, or ought to stand, on the question of war."

During the war years, Debs continued to fight for the working man, even as he had to deal with recurring illnesses. Years of long days and short nights, along with frequent agitation and stress, were taking their toll, so much so that he chose not to run for president in 1916. This left a vacuum in the Socialist Party at a critical time, and it allowed "patriotic preparedness" supporters, such as Victor Berger, the socialist House Representative from Milwaukee and Daniel Hoan, then Mayor of Milwaukee, to gain power in the party, though Debs still remained the party's main leader.

Debs' speeches against the war were not a problem at first, because many Americans, including President Woodrow Wilson, opposed American involvement in the European conflict. However, when America joined the war in 1917, it was expected that all public leaders should get on board and support the war effort.

Wilson

Though it has long been glossed over, Wilson's activities on the home front during the war would make any supporter of civil liberties cringe. In an effort to quell any opposition, Wilson pushed the Espionage Act of 1917, the Immigration Act of 1918, and the Sedition Act of 1918 to tamp down on anyone who even advocated an opinion deemed anti-American, as well as deporting or jailing those deemed to be radicals. Of course, these powers were heavily abused at the drop of a hat, and even the smallest, most innocuous "offense" brought the weight of authority to bear. Dozens of newspapers deemed un-American were deprived of mailing rights and thus the ability to spread their publications, Robert Goldstein found himself imprisoned for producing a movie critical of the British, and Justice Department authorities regularly monitored and harassed anti-war groups, communists, and labor groups that did not sufficiently support the war to the government's liking. Anybody who recently arrived in the country and did not establish their pro-American pro-war bona fides were liable to be deported to Soviet Russia.

As a result, those who spoke out against the war faced possible arrest, and three socialists - Charles Ruthenberg, Charles Baker, and Alfred Wagenknecht - were arrested for criticizing American involvement in the war. At the same time, criticizing the Wilson administration itself could subject citizens to arrest, including Debs, who ran against Wilson in 1912.

C. E. RUTHENBERG.

Ruthenberg

Wagenknecht

Naturally, Debs refused to keep quiet and instead spoke out even louder. On June 16, 1918, he gave the most fateful speech of his life at Nimisilla Park in Canton, Ohio. Debs began his remarks by telling the audience he had been to see Ruthenberg, Baker, and Wagenknecht, and that "over yonder [to the Stark County Workhouse]…three of our most loyal comrades are paying the penalty for their devotion to the cause of the working class…it is extremely dangerous to exercise the constitutional right of free speech in a country fighting to make democracy safe in the world." He went on to declare his support for the others being punished by the government for supporting labor or opposing the war, asserting that none of them were guilty of any real crime. He also insisted that socialism in no way supported Germany or any other nation the United States was fighting against, adding that he himself had "no earthly use for the [nobility] of Germany and have not one particle more use for the [nobility] in the United States."

At the same time, Debs claimed that he opposed the war, just as he would any other, because "[t]he master class has always declared the wars; the subject class has always fought the battles. The master class has had all to gain and nothing to lose, while the subject class has had nothing to gain and all to lose — especially their lives." He later complained that "the purpose of the Allies is exactly the purpose of the Central Powers, and that is the conquest and spoliation of the weaker nations that has always been the purpose of war." He encouraged those in the audience to move from "slavery to freedom and from despotism to democracy, wide as the world" via socialism. He also praised the Bolsheviks in Russia, who he said "shed more heroic blood than any like number of men and women anywhere on earth [to lay] the foundation of the first real democracy that ever drew the breath of life in this world." Debs believed Americans must do the same to oust "the corrupt Republican Party and the still more corrupt Democratic Party," so that in time, "the hour will strike and this great cause triumphant — the greatest in history — will proclaim the emancipation of the working class and the brotherhood of all mankind...It is as vain to resist it as it would be to arrest the sunrise on the morrow."

A picture of Debs delivering the speech in Canton

Though the U.S. Attorney prosecuting Debs questioned whether he had enough of a case to get a conviction, he still had the firebrand socialist arrested for violating the Espionage Act. Unable to show that Debs had, in the Canton speech or in any other, publicly called upon men to avoid the draft, the prosecution claimed that Debs' words would encourage Americans to forsake the loyalty they owed to their country.

During his trial, Debs' attorney called no witnesses to the stand to defend his actions, instead asking that Debs be allowed to address the court on his own behalf. On the one hand, Debs might have been so arrogant as to think that his words alone would sway the court and win his freedom, but given his previous behavior and comments, this seems unlikely. Instead, it seems Debs was so convinced that he would be found guilty that he figured he might as well use the trial as a platform to air his views to a captive audience. In fact, he had noted in Canton, "The trial of a Socialist in a capitalist court is at best a farcical affair. What ghost of a chance had she in a court with a packed jury and a corporation tool on the bench? Not the least in the world. And so she goes to the penitentiary for ten years if they carry out their brutal and disgraceful graceful program. For my part I do not think they will. In fact I feel sure they will not. If the war were over tomorrow the prison doors would open to our people. They simply mean to silence the voice of protest during the war."

Whatever his motives were, he spoke his mind in court on September 11, 1918, telling the court, "I believe in the constitution of the United States. Isn't it strange that we Socialists stand almost alone today in defending the constitution of the United States? The revolutionary fathers who had been oppressed under king rule understood that free speech and free, press and the right of free assemblage by the people were the fundamental principles of democratic government. ... I believe the revolutionary fathers meant just what is here stated that Congress shall make no law abridging the freedom of speech or of the press, or of the right of the people to peaceably assemble, and to petition the government for a redress of grievances. That is the right I exercised at Canton on the 16th day of last June; and for the exercise of that right, I now have to answer to this indictment…I believe in the right of free speech, in war as well as in peace. I would not, under any circumstances, gag the lips of my bitterest enemy. I would under no circumstances suppress free speech. It is far more dangerous to attempt to gag the people than to allow them to speak freely of what is in their hearts. With every drop of blood in my veins I despise Kaiserism, and all that Kaiserism expresses and implies. I have my sympathy with the struggling, suffering people everywhere. It does not make any difference under what flag they were born, or where they live, I have sympathy with them all. I would, if I could, establish a social system that would embrace them all…I am not on trial here. There is an infinitely greater issue that is being tried today in this court, though you may not be conscious of it. American institutions are on trial here before a court of American citizens. The future will tell." Not surprisingly, his words, though eloquent, fell on deaf ears, and the jury convicted him the next day. Later, when given a chance to speak again before his sentencing, he told judge, "I am opposed to the form of our present government; that I am opposed to the social system in which we live; that I believe in the change of both but by perfectly peaceable and orderly means…I am thinking this morning of the men in the mills and factories; I am thinking of the women who, for a paltry wage, are compelled to work out their lives; of the little children who, in this system, are robbed of their childhood, and in their early, tender years, are seized in the remorseless grasp of Mammon, and forced into the industrial dungeons, there to feed the machines while they themselves are being starved body and soul....Your honor, I ask no mercy, I plead for no immunity. I realize that finally the right must prevail. I never more fully comprehended than now the great struggle between the powers of greed on the one hand and upon the other the rising hosts of freedom. I can see the dawn of a better day of humanity. The people are awakening. In due course of time they will come into their own."

Ultimately, Debs concluded, "When the mariner, sailing over tropic seas, looks for relief from his weary watch, he turns his eyes toward the Southern Cross, burning luridly above the tempest-vexed ocean. As the midnight approaches the Southern Cross begins to bend, and the whirling worlds change their places, and with starry finger-points the Almighty marks the passage of Time upon the dial of the universe; and though no bell may beat the glad tidings, the look-out knows that the midnight is passing – that relief and rest are close at hand. Let the people take heart and hope everywhere, for the cross is bending, midnight is passing, and joy cometh with the morning."

The court sentenced Debs to 10 years in prison and forbade him to ever vote again, but the words that he spoke in his sentencing hearing rang in the ears of those who heard them long after he was freed: "Your Honor, years ago I recognized my kinship with all living beings, and I made up my mind that I was not one bit better than the meanest on earth. I said then, and I say now, that while there is a lower class, I am in it, and while there is a criminal element, I am of it, and while there is a soul in prison, I am not free."

Debs was sentenced to serve a decade in the Moundsville State Penitentiary in West Virginia. He arrived there on April 13, 1919, even as his followers, led by Ruthenberg, began to plan ways to get him out. On May 1, the popular "May Day" among socialist circles, unionists, anarchists, socialists and communists joined together for a parade down the streets of Cleveland, Ohio to demand Debs' release and promote Ruthenberg's candidacy for mayor of the city. There were four units marching that day, and as they approached the public square, a group of Victory Liberty Loan workers who had supported the war effort accosted them. Fighting broke out and spread quickly through the immediate area. By the time the city leaders were able to restore order, two people were dead, 40 were injured, and 116 sat in jails around the city.

All the while, Debs' supporters never gave up on him and began a "jail to the White House" campaign for his presidency in 1920. Obviously, there was little hope that he would win, but he did receive more than 900,000 votes, primarily from his fellow socialists and the burgeoning group of communists that were beginning to gather in the country. In 1920, this was less than 3.5% of the popular vote.

A contemporary cartoon making light of Debs' 1920 campaign

While many were campaigning to get Debs elected, others were simply trying to get him out of jail. Perhaps not surprisingly, this was always an uphill battle, because even after the war ended in November 1918, Wilson and his administration targeted radical political opponents with the Palmer Raids, a mass arrest and roundup of thousands of anarchists and labor activists, 500 of which were deported. In 1920, a federal judge would publicly excoriate the raids, writing, "A mob is a mob, whether made up of Government officials acting under instructions from the Department of Justice, or of criminals and loafers and the vicious classes."

The president continued to be personally outraged by Debs' behavior during the war, so much so that he wrote, "While the flower of American youth was pouring out its blood to vindicate the cause of civilization, this man, Debs, stood behind the lines sniping, attacking, and denouncing them....This man was a traitor to his country and he will never be pardoned during my administration." When Attorney General A. Mitchell Palmer asked Wilson to pardon Debs because of poor health in 1921, Wilson denied it. According to Lincoln Steffens, one of those fighting on Debs' behalf, "President Wilson received and read on his boat our amnesty memorandum, but he rejected the idea of it sharply, totally. He was in a fighting, acting mood, bitter and executive. And the American people were not ready for anything like peace."

Palmer

Debs also appealed his case through the courts, and it eventually reached the Supreme Court. In *Debs v. United States*, the Supreme Court studied transcripts of his speeches and ruled that, although Debs never explicitly encouraged his listeners to avoid the draft, he did imply that they should do so by praising those who had. In his opinion, Justice Oliver Wendell Holmes, Jr. wrote that Debs' case was similar to that of *Schenck v. United States*, in which the Court had ruled in favor of the government.

The jailing of Debs is almost universally condemned today, and it was even controversial at the time. One early 20th century journalist, Heywood Broun, noted, "I imagine that now it would be difficult to find many to defend the jailing of Debs. But at the time of the trial he received little support outside the radical ranks. The problem involved was not simple. I hated the thing they did to Debs even at the time, and I was not then a pacifist...Free speech is about as good a cause as the world has ever known. But, like the poor, it is always with us and gets shoved aside in favor of things which seem at some given moment more vital. They never are more vital. Not when you look back at them from a distance. When the necessity of free speech is most important we shut it off. Everybody favors free speech in the slack moments when no axes are being ground."

Final Years

"The working class must be emancipated by the working class.

Woman must be given her true place in society by the working class.

Child labor must be abolished by the working class.

Society must be reconstructed by the working class.

The working class must be employed by the working class.

The fruits of labor must be enjoyed by the working class.

War, bloody war, must be ended by the working class." – Debs, 1904

Debs remained in prison throughout Wilson's second term, but his spirit continued to thrive, and his friends continued to fight for his freedom, as well as that of others. Steffens later recalled, "It looked better when Harding was president. After he had been in office awhile I went to him with a similar proposition [of amnesty], and to be sure of my ground, I sounded first a small number of governors to see if they would join in a general , act of clemency for war and labor prisoners. Right away I got the reaction familiar to me: the politician governors would pardon their prisoners if the president would pardon his; the better men, the good, business governors, were most unwilling. Well, Harding was a politician; rumor had it that he was a sinner. President Harding heard me out, his handsome face expressing his willingness and his doubt. He nodded, smiled, wagged his head. 'Make peace at home,' I said. 'We've got it abroad. Let all the prisoners go who are in jail for fighting for labor, for peace, for-anything. Let 'em all out, with a proclamation, you and the governors.'"

According to Steffens, Harding's reply was positive but cautious. "'That's all right,' he said, 'for fellows like you and me, but they won't let me do it.' He had the case of Eugene V. Debs, the socialist leader, before him; we all knew that, and I had asked his permission to visit Debs in Atlanta. 'I am going to pardon Debs,' he said."

Later, Steffens returned to Harding's office to find the new president "had in his hand a typewritten paper which he pushed at me. 'Here, look at this.' It was a declaration his attorney general had dictated for Debs to sign when pardoned, a dirt-eating promise. 'What would you do about that?' Harding asked, and when I looked up from reading it and said, with some feeling, that I would not pardon any man who would subscribe to such a statement, he nodded. 'I thought so,' he muttered, and he crumpled the paper and dropped it. He pardoned Debs without any humiliating conditions."

Harding

The manner in which Debs was ultimately pardoned on Christmas Day in 1921 was rather interesting. According to historian Bill Kauffmann, "Harding lacked Wilson's intellect as well as his mean streak. The kindly Buckeye asked his venal Attorney General Harry Daugherty to meet with Debs in March 1921, so the prisoner was shipped northward on a train to Washington, where he met with Daugherty and Harding gofer Jess Smith…These Doublemint twins of GOP corruption were charmed by Debs. Although Daugherty opposed a pardon, he pronounced the Socialist 'sincere, gentle, and tender,' and the solicitous Smith even ran into a drugstore to buy a bundle of quill toothpicks for Debs after the prisoner complained of jail-house plaque…Among those pleading Debs' case was his Socialist Party heir, Norman Thomas, who by extraordinary coincidence had once been a dollar-a-week paperboy delivering Harding's [newspaper, the *Ohio Marion*] *Star*. Thomas, who regarded the President as a genial Babbitt…visited Harding twice in the White House. The homeboys reminisced about good old Marion before Thomas asked, 'Is it not a splendid thing that a country should have men brave enough to speak their minds even when they are in a minority?' Harding agreed."

Daugherty

Thus, Harding agreed to sign the pardon, but the process hit a snag. Kauffmann explained, "He intended to release Debs on July 4, but the American Legion protested so vociferously that he delayed the pardon from the anniversary of American liberty to the season of Christian charity." Even when Harding pardoned Debs in December 1921, he claimed, "He was by no means as rabid and outspoken in his expressions as many others, and but for his prominence and the resulting far-reaching effect of his words, very probably might not have received the sentence he did. He is an old man, not strong physically. He is a man of much personal charm and impressive personality, which…make him a dangerous man calculated to mislead the unthinking and affording excuse for those with criminal intent."

Steffens described Debs' reaction to going free: "When I visited Debs at Atlanta and told him what was coming, he was not elated. He was a happy man in prison. He loved everybody there, and everybody loved him…Debs wanted to hear 'all about the Russian Revolution,' the outrages of which he had denounced. It was not socialist, he pleaded…Like so many reds who rejected Bolshevism, Debs the socialist could not abide the violence, bloodshed, tyranny."

A picture of Debs being released

If Debs was not happy about his release, his followers were elated, as were his fellow prisoners. According to journalist Howard Zinn, "Debs had won the hearts of his fellow prisoners in Atlanta. He had fought for them in a hundred ways and refused any special privileges for himself…On the day of his release, the warden ignored prison regulations and opened every cellblock to allow more than 2,000 inmates to gather in front of the main jail building to say goodbye to Eugene Debs. As he started down the walkway from the prison, a roar went up and he turned, tears streaming down his face, and stretched out his arms to the other prisoners." A fellow prisoner, Sam Moore, remembered, "As miserable as I was, I would defy fate with all its cruelty as long as Debs held my hand, and I was the most miserably happiest man on Earth when I knew he was going home Christmas."

Upon his release, Debs became one of the few people to ever walk out of prison and into the White House, for President Harding invited him to come for a visit. According to Debs, upon meeting him, Harding said, "Well, I have heard so damned much about you, Mr. Debs, that I am now very glad to meet you personally." When asked by reporters how the brief meeting had gone, and whether he still harbored any political aspirations himself, Debs replied, "Mr. Harding appears to me to be a kind gentle man, one whom I believe possesses humane impulses. We understand each other perfectly. As for the White House — well, gentlemen, my personal preference is to live privately as a humble citizen in my cottage at Terre Haute. "When a reporter reminded him that he was, in fact, no longer a citizen according to the disenfranchisement clause of his sentencing, Debs assured him, "That is a matter of no import to me. The sovereignty of my citizenship resulted in my imprisonment. The government has made me a citizen of the world in fact. I am happy to be a Citizen of the World."

Debs noted that "because I am a 66-year-old ex-convict, who happened to be five times candidate for President of the United States, I shall do nothing at all to enhance that curiosity. I would not under any circumstances accept a single lecture engagement if I felt that I was to be exhibited like a sideshow. If there is nothing more to me than that, then I might just as well go into eclipse right now…It is undoubtedly true that never before was such a rare opportunity offered me to write my message into the newspapers as there has been offered since I left Atlanta prison. Yet I believe the writing of the prison articles is taking a legitimate advantage of their offer. If the capitalist system can stand for what I have to say in its newspapers, I am willing to be exploited to that extent."

A picture of Debs leaving the White House

To his credit, Debs devoted the remaining years of his life trying to correct some of the misconceptions held by socialists and others about what the movement entailed. Speaking of the story finally released about the deaths of the remaining Romanov royals near the end of World War I, he declared, "My blood boiled when I read the other day of the heinous murder of the czar, his wife and daughters. The crime was of such a revolting nature that it confounds the intelligent sensibilities of anybody who calls himself a Socialist. The Russians excuse it not only on the ground that the czar and his family alive might be menacing to the revolution, but also justify their crime by pointing to the fact that the reigning imperialists were likewise guilty of brutal and hideous murders of Russian workers. For myself, there is no excuse for Socialists and free men to resurrect the archaic, Mosaic law. Socialists should set an example by treating their opponents with kindness and consideration and not resorting to the gallows, the knout and the pistol, as is the custom of their adversaries. I believe with Thomas Paine, that we should 'destroy the king, but save the man.'"

It is no surprise, then, that in spite of pressure from those around him, Debs refused to join the growing American Communist Party.

In 1924, Debs was surprised and flattered to learn that Finnish socialist leader Karl H. Wiik had nominated him for the Nobel Peace Prize, but for the most part, he spent the last months of his life ill and depressed over what he perceived to be the failure of his life's work. In the fall of 1926, he entered the Lindlahr Sanitarium in Elmhurst, Illinois, in the hopes that rest and good food might cure him, but the efforts were to no avail, and he died there on October 20, 1926 of heart failure. His wife had his body cremated and buried at the Highland Lawn Cemetery in Terre Haute.

In the obituary to the late socialist leader, Broun wrote for the *New Your World*, "Eugene Debs was a beloved figure and a tragic one. All his life he led lost causes. He captured the intense loyalty of a small section of our people, but I think that he affected the general thought of his time to a slight degree. Very few recognized him for what he was. It became the habit to speak of him as a man molded after the manner of Lenin or Trotsky. And that was a grotesque misconception. People were constantly overlooking the fact that Debs was a Hoosier, a native product in every strand of him. He was a sort of Whitcomb Riley turned politically minded. It does not seem to me that he was a great man. At least he was not a great intellect. ... By any test such as that Debs was great. Certainly he had character. There was more of goodness in him than bubbled up in any other American of his day. He had some humor, or otherwise a religion might have been built up about him, for he was thoroughly Messianic. And it was a strange quirk which set this gentle, sentimental Middle-Westerner in the leadership of a party often fierce and militant...Though not a Christian by any precise standard, Debs was the Christian-Socialist type...He did feel that wrongs could be righted by touching the compassion of the world...Of cold, logical Marxism, Debs possessed very little. He was never the brains of his party. I never met him, but I read many of his speeches, and most of them seemed to be second-rate utterances. But when his great moment came a miracle occurred. Debs made a speech to the judge and jury at Columbus after his conviction, and to me it seems one of the most beautiful and moving passages in the English language. He was for that one afternoon touched with inspiration. If anybody told me that tongues of fire danced upon his shoulders as he spoke, I would believe it.... Something was in Debs, seemingly, that did not come out unless you saw him. I'm told that even those speeches of his which seemed to any reader indifferent stuff, took on vitality from his presence."

Broun then concluded, "I've said that it did not seem to me that Debs was a great man in life, but he will come to greatness by and by. There are in him the seeds of symbolism. He was a sentimental Socialist, and that line has dwindled all over the world. Radicals talk now in terms of men and guns and power, and unless you get in at the beginning of the meeting and orient yourself, this could just as well be Security Leaguers or any other junkers in session. The Debs idea will not die. To be sure, it was not his first at all. He carried on an older tradition. It will come to pass. There can be a brotherhood of man."

Online Resources

Other books about 19th century America by Charles River Editors

Other books about 20th century America by Charles River Editors

Other books about Debs on Amazon

Further Reading

Bernard J. Brommel, Eugene V. Debs: Spokesman for Labor and Socialism. Chicago: Charles H. Kerr Publishing Co., 1978.

McAlister Coleman, Eugene V. Debs: A Man Unafraid. New York: Greenberg, 1930.

J. Robert Constantine (ed.), Gentle Rebel: Letters of Eugene V. Debs. Urbana: University of Illinois Press, 1995.

J. Robert Constantine (ed.), Letters of Eugene V. Debs. In Three Volumes. Urbana: University of Illinois Press, 1990.

Ray Ginger, The Bending Cross: A Biography of Eugene Victor Debs. Rutgers University Press: 1949.

Herbert M. Morais and William Cahn, Eugene Debs: The Story of a Fighting American. New York: International Publishers, 1948.

Nick Salvatore, Eugene V. Debs: Citizen and Socialist. Reprinted by University of Illinois Press, 1984.

Irving Stone. Adversary in the House. New York: Doubleday, 1947. —Historical fiction.

Free Books by Charles River Editors

We have brand new titles available for free most days of the week. To see which of our titles are currently free, click on this link.

Discounted Books by Charles River Editors

We have titles at a discount price of just 99 cents everyday. To see which of our titles are currently 99 cents, click on this link.

Made in the USA
Middletown, DE
08 December 2019